CITY OF TRURO
MAIN LINE CENTENARY

by Michael Rutherford

The author doing his stint as fireman on City of Truro *in Utrecht, Holland during the NS 150 celebrations (NS stands for Nederlandse Spoorwegen). The exhibition locomotives were waiting to leave the depot, coupled together. The special train was also waiting for a signal and was hauled by two German locomotives owned by Dutch preservationists. They were West German standard class 65 2-8-4T No. 65.018. built in 1956 and a 1944 built 'Kriegslok', No. 52.3879.*
(Richard Gibbon)

AUTHOR'S PREFACE

This is the fourth National Collection steam locomotive to have been described in a book of this form, following *Mallard: The Record Breaker, Duchess of Hamilton: Ultimate in Pacific Power* and *Green Arrow and the LNER V2 Class.* I have been author or co-author of them all and have also been privileged to have been a member of the support crew with them on many occasions of main line running.

Such intimacy soon brings an often much-needed dose of reality to the proceedings when it is necessary to clean ashpans, smokeboxes and gratebars, crawl about inside the machinery to oil it or clean accumulated filth – especially from wheels, frames and running gear – tasks which could often be made considerably more difficult due to wind, rain and cold!

Somehow memories of *City of Truro* never seem to conjure up such spells of hardship amongst all the good times; it always *seems* to have been sunny when it has been working, often with trips from York to the seaside at Scarborough. Perhaps because it is a relatively small locomotive, cleaning has been easy and polishing the copper and brass a pleasure especially when the outcome is such an attractive sight.

I saw *City of Truro* after its first liberation from museum confinement, once dead on shed and once in steam. The livery that had been applied in 1957 – and quickly criticised as incorrect by the cognoscenti – seemed a little 'loud' in the eyes of an avid schoolboy spotter, used to BR standard green or, more often than not, black and the whole business seemed somewhat quaint and out of the mainstream. In those days on British Railways, class 8 steam power far outnumbered the new main line diesels on express passenger train workings and attracted much of our attention. It was also difficult to associate that machine with the legendary exploits of the 'Cities' as related in O.S. Nock's gripping tales of Edwardian days.

Following its return to display as a museum exhibit (this time at Swindon) in a more sombre livery, I would try to give it a few minutes on the occasional visit to Swindon but I have to admit that I was rather more attracted to 'Dean Goods' 0-6-0 No. 2516 and *Lode Star.*

The second removal – in July 1984 – to the workshops of the Severn Valley Railway at Bridgnorth was, I confess, a move of which I was critical at the time, taking a rather over-serious, curatorial view of things. Critical, that is, until the old girl arrived at York early on the morning of 1st August 1986 and I became part of the support crew from the beginning.

It is quite remarkable how quickly the engine endeared itself to everyone and also how little coal and water – especially the latter – it used when compared with the large engines undertaking the same work; the 'Scarborough Spa

Express' for example. The theatre of operations of *City of Truro* following its second escape from museum display was more extensive than the first, even involving a trip to the European mainland as a great ambassador for the National Railway Museum.

Now that preparations for a third resurrection are under way I have no doubts that the necessary work should be undertaken so that this grand old locomotive can be seen on the main line again. It could be the last time; much new safety and other legislation can make things difficult for the older machines to comply and present-day costs are such that special trains need to be of maximum size and as full as possible to be paying propositions. This tends to lead to the requirement for a Pacific.

We should therefore make the most of the opportunity that once again will give us the chance to travel behind this wonderful engine on some of Britain's main line railways.

An earlier book about *City of Truro* was first published in 1985 and reprinted in 1992 (see further reading list). I have tried not to cover all the same topics as that work and hope that this volume will be seen as a worthwhile supplement.

Michael Rutherford
York, 2003

ACKNOWLEDGEMENTS

I would like to thank Bill Greenwood of the Friends of the National Railway Museum for asking me to write this book in the first place and for his patience. Thanks also to Mike Blakemore for correcting my grammar and punctuation and offering a number of suggestions. There would be no book without the pictures and I am grateful to John Edgington and John Gilks, Mike Blakemore (again), Richard Gibbon and Ron White of Colour-Rail. Finally, without the material accessible in the Library of the NRM the task of researching historical events would have been much more difficult, so many thanks to the Librarian Phil Atkins, and his staff.

INTRODUCTION

Old steam locomotives that have escaped the cutters' torch are not necessarily the ones that, with hindsight, we might have selected and the further we go back in time the more we find engines which have survived due to plain luck or for a spurious reason. On the other hand many locomotives that were thought to have been 'saved' were eventually scrapped, more often than not to clear space in railway-owned premises, there being no railway-specific museums in which to display them and the idea of a *preserved* railway had to wait until the aftermath of the Second World War and the pioneers of the Talyllyn Railway Preservation Society.

Whilst a *national* railway museum had been mooted when Queen Victoria was on the throne, it was to be 80 years before the idea became a reality and when it did, it was to be built on the foundations laid by a group of North Eastern Railway officers in the final years of the existence of that company. Well aware of its own unique roots with the steam railway pioneers, the NER had accumulated a considerable collection of relics and these proved useful in public relations exercises both for the company and in emphasizing the solid foundations of the north east region's industrial base.

Fortunately the LNER, successor to the NER, continued to develop the museum (set up at York) and interest in Britain's railway history was enhanced by the 1925 Railway Centenary celebrations held at Darlington. Although on LNER territory, Darlington briefly became home to locomotives and rolling stock from all the 'Big Four' companies and a grand procession of 54 locomotive, railcars and complete trains ran on a section of the old Stockton & Darlington Railway past a grandstand erected near Urlay Nook, about 3½ miles west of Eaglescliffe. The cavalcade was complemented with a large exhibition in Faverdale wagon shops (Darlington) and the whole medley was opened by the Duke and Duchess of York (later King George VI and Queen Elizabeth).

The celebrations were perhaps more elaborate than they might have been and were held in July rather than the more historically correct September because the International Railway Congress Association held its five-yearly Congress in London that year and the exhibition and cavalcade became part of the programme. The centenary thus became more than just a local or even national event but an international one and was soon to lead to many more in other countries.

It gave a great boost to the whole concept of saving some of Britain's railway heritage for display in a publicly accessible museum and it was not long before locomotives were being offered to the York Museum for display which had no associations with the LNER or the North East of England.

For example, London, Brighton & South Coast Railway 0-4-2 No. 214 *Gladstone*, withdrawn in 1927, was given by the Southern Railway to the Stephenson Locomotive Society on the understanding that the latter organisation would fund cosmetic restoration to its original appearance. (The cost was a mere £150!). After appearing in a couple of exhibitions in London and Brighton in 1927, it was offered to the Science Museum at South Kensington but room could not be found and so it was accepted at York to where it was moved. Similarly, Grand Junction Railway No. 49 *Columbine*, an old 'Crewe-type' 2-2-2, was sent to York from Crewe in 1934, presented by the London Midland & Scottish Railway.

For many years *Columbine* was described as being the first locomotive to have been built at Crewe Works. Indeed it is possibly the reason why York originally accepted it for exhibition. That it was in fact the twentieth locomotive built at Crewe (in July 1845, the first having been No. 32 *Tamerlane* in October 1843) *might* have seen it lost to us. Now, of course, such an idea would horrify everyone. The importance of a 'Crewe-type' locomotive to the National Collection is such that *Columbine* is now proudly exhibited in the Science Museum itself.

Similarly, the Great Western Railway 4-4-0 *City of Truro* was preserved and exhibited at York because of a legendary feat of performance on 9th May 1904 when, it was later claimed, the engine achieved a maximum speed of 102.3 mph, the first steam locomotive to break through the magic 100 mph barrier. More recently writers have claimed that on that date *City of Truro* became the first vehicle in the world to achieve a speed of 100 mph and that it was … "the fastest machine built by man".

Even a cursory glance at the known facts reveals that there simply is not enough evidence to demonstrate that 100 mph was achieved and from what we *do* know, the power required for the final acceleration would be at least twice as much as *City of Truro* was capable of. The spurious accuracy of the 102.3 mph only obfuscates the whole affair.

As far as 100 mph by rail is concerned, in Germany in 1901 a Bo-Bo electric locomotive reached 101 mph (162 km/hr) and in 1903 an electric railcar of Siemens manufacture achieved 124.8 mph (200.8 km/hr). A similar vehicle, built to AEG design, in the same series of tests peaked at 130.7 mph (210.4 km/hr) thus running faster than *Mallard's* 1938 record for steam even *before* the *City of Truro* escapade! It should be pointed out that the speeds quoted above were measured using accurate instrumentation rather than relying on a hand-held mechanical stopwatch allied to human observation of quarter-mile posts.

Having tempered the romance with some hard reality, it would be well to emphasise that without the record run it is most unlikely that this or any other 'City' would have been saved and that would have been a very great pity because that class (together with the preceding 'Atbaras') were the fastest British locomotives of the day – speeds in the 90s were recorded on several occasions – and were probably the fastest non-superheated slide-valve designs ever. There is no doubt that in original condition *City of Truro* was capable of reaching 100 mph down Wellington bank; whether it did so on 9th May 1904 will always be a matter of endless speculation.

The 'new' Great Western began to take shape in the late 1890s. Track was laid and quadrupled where traffic was heavy and in order to run long non-stop journeys, water troughs were laid down and new sets of coaches built, with lavatories and corridors throughout. The first loco- motives built specifically for such express passenger services were the twenty 4-4-0s of the 'Badminton' class introduced from 1897. Here No. 3297 Earl Cawdor *picks up water from Goring troughs with a down South Wales express in 1898.*

(L. & G.R.P.)

That speed however was not made public immediately; the *record* was the running of the Ocean Mails Special over the whole distance between Millbay Docks, Plymouth, and Paddington and, combined with a Blue Riband journey by the *Kronprinz Wilhelm*, resulted in an overall record for the mails between New York and London.

The main features of the 'City' design combined some very traditional elements, such as double frames and fly-cracks with one of the first examples of the type of tapered Belpaire boiler first introduced to Britain by George Churchward on the GWR which was built in its thousands, in various sizes, by that company, the LMSR (taken there by William Stanier in 1932) and by British Railways in the standard classes. There are very good reasons why the 'City' design was as it was and why it was only a 4-4-0. We will return to design details shortly but first we must put GWR developments into a proper historical context.

THE BROAD GAUGE LEGACY

In the late 1840s at the end of a period that became known as the 'Gauge War', the Great Western Railway, laid to Brunel's broad gauge of seven feet, was running the fastest express trains in the world at speeds not equalled in regular service elsewhere for a quarter of a century.

Such speeds were, however, short-lived because they could not be justified economically. The wear and tear on locomotives and track were great and there were many limitations to the materials available and also to the precision of the large machine tools then in use. In those days too, coke was the main fuel (occasionally shared with coal in special fireboxes) and was very expensive. The later, specialised lubricating oils had not been developed and most lubrication was effected using rendered animal fats such as tallow. Nevertheless events from this era became legendary and grist to the mill of Paddington's later publicity machine (as of course did *City of Truro's* record run of 1904).

During the 1850s the company took over standard gauge lines north of Birmingham. The latter were built to mixed gauge and the third rail was laid south from Oxford until it reached Paddington in 1861, although broad gauge trains worked north as far as Wolverhampton (the northern limit of the broad gauge) until the autumn of 1868. The GWR amalgamated with the West Midland Railway series of lines as from 1st August 1863 when there was a considerable amount of friction at board level and shortly after, the former Locomotive Superintendent, Sir Daniel Gooch (knighted for his part in laying the first trans-Atlantic cable), was brought back as the company's chairman. There had been a second 'railway mania' in the early 1860s but a financial panic in 1866 saw many lose their money and the GWR's bank Overend, Gurney & Co (known as 'Bankers to the Empire') collapsed leaving the railway company in a precarious financial position for many years. The broad gauge locomotive stock of GWR reached 419 (its peak) in 1866 when the standard gauge total was 407 but by the end of 1884 the totals were 200 and 1,805 respectively. Thus the standard gauge totally dominated the railways activities but the retention of the broad gauge on the old main line and in the West Country tends to leave an impression otherwise.

The only major works undertaken from 1866 to the end of the century (apart from various amalgamations) were the Severn Tunnel – opened in 1886 – and the gradual quadrupling of the original main line out of Paddington. There was a considerable amount of mixed gauge track in service and its maintenance was very costly. With the complete elimination of the broad gauge in sight it was not deemed economical to lay mixed gauge on new, cross-sleepered track with stronger rails and so the trackwork, in the main, remained of the longitudinal-sleepered variety to which bridge rails were bolted.

This type of formation – Isambard Kingdom Brunel's 'baulk road' was difficult to keep in correct alignment with regard to level and caused locomotives to 'roll' as they ran along, this being exacerbated by the out-of-balance forces produced by all two-cylinder engines with cranks set at 90°. This phenomenon was worse on standard gauge track laid on baulk road and even more so

In September 1902, 'Atbara' No. 3705 Mauritius *was rebuilt with a larger boiler with a tapered barrel and rearward taper to the firebox sides and top. This was the 'standard No. 4' boiler and the resulting combination became the prototype 'City'. It is seen here in later years after fitting with a superheater, top-feed and a copper-capped chimney.*
(Atlantic collection)

The boiler for Mauritius came from an order for twenty for a batch of 'Aberdare' 2-6-0 goods engines. These can be considered the freight version of the 'City' class. No. 2666 shown here was built in September 1902, the same month that No. 3705 was converted.

(Author's collection)

for mixed gauge formations where it was impossible to keep three rails properly aligned. Baulk road was extremely rigid and is why almost all broad gauge engines were erected on sandwich frames which were resilient and absorbed some of the bumps. Very long open plate springs were used which gave a good soft ride and were only displaced on driving axles where volute springs and iron and rubber composite springs were employed; sometimes there were combinations of different springs in some places.

Many features of broad gauge practice were carried over into standard gauge locomotive construction including sandwich frames but double plate frames were found to perform similar functions. This construction continued into the twentieth century in order to deal with the unique legacy of Brunel's type of trackwork. Even the old main line was not completely relaid with heavy-section bull-head track throughout until 1897.

Until Churchward's larger 4-6-0s had been built in sufficient numbers, the 'Cities' were hard-worked. There were ten built from new, ten from 'Atbaras' and 17 of the twenty 'Badmintons' were fitted with No. 4 boilers for a few years but were later given smaller boilers. 'Badminton' No. 3310 Waterford is seen here as a 'City' (it was the first so fitted) with an up express at Saltford, west of Bath.

(Author's collection)

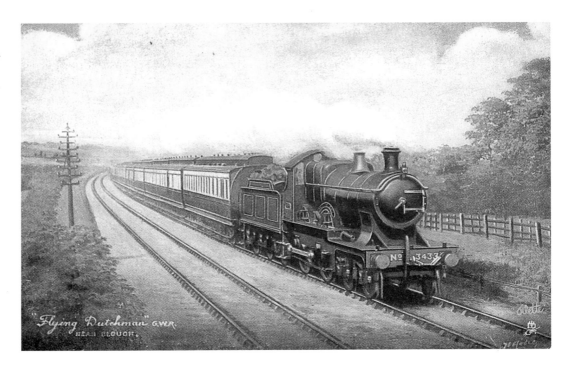

With the double-frame arrangement there were four bearings on the driving (crank) axle, giving generous surfaces and each was separately sprung (on the 'Atbaras' and 'Cities' the outside springs were overhung and the inside, under-hung) and could be adjusted independently. Crank axles on large coupled double-framed locomotives were known to have a higher rate of fracture (this was not, apparently, the case with 'single-wheelers') but in the late 1890s Swindon, like many other works, introduced the built-up crank axle. Special steels and precision grinding machines made this possible and flaws in such assemblies could be spotted and the axle rebuilt before complete failure occurred.

Along with the 'Atbaras' and 'Cities' (and the smaller 'Bulldog') 4-4-0s, 81 double-framed goods engines, the 2-6-0 'Aberdares' were built during the same period and incorporated many common components. It should be perhaps be remembered that the works (and stores etc.) at Swindon were geared up to deal with double-framed engines, both new-build and repairs, and that the vast new 'A' erecting shop, intended for Churchward's more advanced ideas, was still being built and equipped at this time.

City of Truro *in Swindon Works yard with a Stephenson Locomotive Society special on 16th June 1957.*

(T.J. Edgington)

An immaculate No. 3440 at Southampton Terminus. City of Truro *worked service trains on the Didcot, Newbury and Southampton line when first returned to working order.* (B.J. Swain/Colour-Rail BRW 249)

City of Truro *at Newbury on 9th July 1957 with the 12.42 pm Didcot-Southampton.* (T.J. Edgington)

On 16th June 1957 No. 3440 worked a Stephenson Locomotive Society special to Swindon. It is seen here entering Birmingham, Snow Hill. (T.J. Edgington)

Towards the end of the second restoration to working order, on the Severn Valley Railway, City of Truro *was painted – partially and as a spoof – in British Railway lined black livery. It caused a considerable amount of ink to be expended in letters to enthusiasts' magazines.*

(G.F. Bannister/Colour-Rail P148)

The first main line outing for City of Truro, *in October 1985, was a 'mystery tour' organised by SLOA. It was photographed after leaving Gloucester, hauling the Inter-City excursion coaches in 'raspberry ripple' livery.* (Colour-Rail P149)

Once construction of the new, big standard engines was under way, Churchward looked at the possibility of a series of light, inside-frame, inside-cylinder 4-4-0 and 2-6-0 classes of modest power to replace older designs on secondary lines. However his plan to use the standard 10in piston valves, valve gear and other components of the bigger designs was thwarted when it was found that there was insufficient room if the standard taper boilers were to be fitted and so between May 1906 and January 1910 further batches of double-framed engines were built. Although this policy has been criticised in recent years as anachronistic, it should be pointed out that the very last batch – the 'Bird' series of 'Bulldogs' – built in 1909-10 averaged around 40 years of useful service each, all becoming part of British Railways stock in 1948.

Later in the day the train was photographed near Magor, west of Newport (Mon.) (Colour-Rail P150)

One of the myths of the City of Truro's *record run was that gold bullion was being carried on the train but bullion was very heavy and carried in special vans, with reinforced floors, extra-strong bogies and special locks, with doors on one side only. The vans weighed 23 tons even without any cargo. Two are seen here behind Churchward 4-4-2 No. 183 Redgauntlet leaving Paddington with a down express. The vans may be returning empty or are perhaps destined for the Birmingham Mint which had rail access via Snow Hill Tunnel.*
(L.G.R.P./Author's collection)

A further criticism, that double-frame construction was more expensive than single, does not stand up either. The 'Cities' of 1903 built to Swindon LOT 141 cost £1,957 apiece whereas the equivalent inside-framed 'County' 4-4-0s of 1904 built to LOT 149 were £2,057 each. These were not high prices by anyone's standards. For example the Caledonian Railway '140' class 4-4-0s built at St. Rollox to order Y72 in 1904 cost £3,044; the London & South Western Railway built a total of forty L11 class 4-4-0s between 1903 and 1907 and costs averaged £2,230 apiece. Inevitably private builders prices were even higher. The South Eastern & Chathan Railway ordered further examples of the 'D' class 4-4-0 from Vulcan Foundry at £3,345 each, Robert Stephenson & Co at £3,320 and Dübs & Co. at £3,370, all in 1902.

City of Truro, as No. 3717, in final condition and still coupled to a tender wider (3500 gallons) than that attached at any time once withdrawn, takes a rest at Shrewsbury.
(T.J. Edgington collection)

Four 'Cities' being cut up in Swindon scrapyard. They are believed to be four that were all withdrawn together in April 1929 – 3702 Halifax, 3707 Malta, 3716 City of London and 3719 City of Exeter.

(Author's collection)

G.J. CHURCHWARD AND GREAT WESTERN LOCOMOTIVE DEVELOPMENT

The 'Cities' were designed for a purpose and within certain constraints of the time (we have seen why double-frames were used, for example) but before looking at the changing circumstances and services of the GWR we should take a look at the background of the man responsible for the design – George Jackson Churchward.

George Churchward was born at Stoke Gabriel, South Devon on 31st January 1857 into a long-established family of yeoman stock. Although enjoying country pursuits to the end of his life, George seems not to have been attracted to the land or the sea by way of career. An ability at mathematics and an interest in things mechanical led him, in 1873 at the age of 16, to a pupillage with John Wright, the Locomotive, Carriage and Wagon Superintendent of the South Devon, Cornwall and West Cornwall Railways. The works were at Newton Abbot, only ten miles from his home.

In the late 1870s the Great Western began to amalgamate with its broad gauge allies in the West Country and George was moved to Swindon in 1876 to complete his apprenticeship. He began drawing office work in 1877 and a little later was actively involved in the Great Western automatic vacuum brake development. His first move up the management ladder was his appointment as assistance manager of the carriage and wagon works; he took over as manager in 1885.

During this period he was involved with the conversion of a great deal of broad gauge rolling stock to standard gauge as well as fitting in an increasing amount of new construction.

His abilities as a production engineer-manager soon shone through (he built a good team of subordinates) and this was complemented by his inventive abilities when he developed the 'O.K.' oil axlebox for carriages and wagons, a feature that was to be an essential detail in the running of fast, long-distance trains and the basic form of which lasted until the final rolling stock, built to GWR designs was completed in the 1950s.

Having shown his abilities under pressure, he was appointed assistant to the Works Manager, Samuel Carlton in 1895 and took on the senior role the following year when Carlton died. The latter was a man whose life would have been a prize for a modern oral historian. He began his career at the Edge Hill works of the Grand Junction Railway before moving to Crewe; the Vulcan Foundry works at Newton-le-Willows followed, then the GWR's Wolverhampton works in 1855. He was Works Manager at Swindon from 1864 until 1896 and he had overall control of all the shops. William Dean, Churchward's boss and Locomotive, Carriage and Wagon Superintendent, divided the authority and Churchward concentrated on the locomotive works while L. R. Thomas was given carriages and wagons.

City of Truro *in the original Railway Museum at Queen Street, York.*

(T.J. Edgington collection)

Clearly there was much to be done and Dean's health was poor (a situation of which he was aware); he was only 56 while Churchward was 39 but unmarried and had no domestic concerns to distract him. Once he had settled in to his new post, Dean appointed him as his Chief Assistant on 27th July 1897, new duties which he took up whilst continuing to run the locomotive works.

Up to this period most Great Western expresses were hauled by small six-wheeled engines; 2-2-2s and 2-4-0s. In the west beyond Exeter almost all traffic was in the hands of tank engines. Introducing bigger engines was hampered by the lack of suitable turntables; the existing ones could not be replaced overnight. Two major accidents made it imperative to make some progress however.

Dean's biggest 2-2-2s were the '3001' class introduced in January 1892 and intended to supersede the 'Rover' class broad gauge engines when the time came. On 16th September 1892, No. 3021 *Wigmore Castle* broke its leading axle and was derailed *inside* Box Tunnel. Fortunately the potential catastrophe was unrealised but the accident led to a rapid return to the drawing board; drawings were prepared for a new batch and a 4-2-2 was schemed out – the '3031' or 'Achilles' class.

Fitting in a conventional bogie was not possible. Dean, on his later, larger designs, had adopted William Stroudley's layout of slide valves, sloping downward from the horizontal *underneath* the cylinders. With this arrangement, when steam was shut off, the valves were no longer held against their faces by steam pressure, and friction and wear were reduced whilst lubrication was continued via the steam ports. It also gave good access to the steam chests from a pit and generous and fairly direct exhaust passages.

Fortunately Dean had been developing his suspension bogie for carriages and this was adapted for locomotive use with success, being fitted to new batches of the 'singles' with earlier engines rebuilt to conform. Four odd engines awaiting renewal had been earmarked to form a class of large express 2-4-0s but the design was changed to 4-4-0s with driving wheels of 7ft diameter. They were handsome machines and obviously from the same stable as the bogie singles but were disappointing in performance and no more were built, whereas 49 more singles followed them.

The second accident occurred on 16th April 1895 when a pair of '3521' class 0-4-4Ts left the track at Doublebois in Cornwall when hauling an express. The Inspecting Officer at the public enquiry which followed condemned the locomotives as totally unsuitable for express passenger traffic and indicated that most similar designs of tank engines were unsuitable for such work. As already noted, the lines west of Exeter, and more particularly west of Newton Abbot, used tank engines almost exclusively and turntables were very small.

Although a 2-4-0 tender engine was considered at first it was quickly decided that bogie engines would be *de rigueur* for the future and so a 4-4-0 was quickly designed with the first two being wheeled out of Swindon Works in May 1895, No. 3252 *Duke of Cornwall* and No. 3253 *Pendennis Castle*. Because of the turntable problem, very small tenders of only 11ft wheelbase and a water capacity of only 2,000 gallons were supplied. Even so, outriders on the turntables were needed in some places to turn these locomotives. The bogies of the first 40 engines and the first 25 tenders were fitted with

Snow Hill Station, Birmingham on 25th August 1957 and an SLS special for Swindon and Eastleigh. City of
Truro *is temporarily fitted with a short safety-valve bonnet, acquired at Caerphilly works after the original was
damaged under the coaling stage at Llanelli. It was soon replaced.* (T.J. Edgington)

*Later in the day – at Eastleigh – note that the special has run into the works' yard and reduced all unnecessary
walking!* (T.J. Edgington)

Mansell-type wheels with solid wood centres made of teak segments, further measures to combat the remaining main line installations of 'baulk road'.

Competition and the rapidly increasing amount of traffic highlighted the need for the GWR not only to modernise the locomotive stock but also considerably supplement it. The problem was that there was not enough workshop capacity at either Swindon or Wolverhampton. It had not been company policy to purchase locomotives from outside suppliers and in any case by the late 1890s waiting lists and delivery times were long (not aided by strikes in the engineering industry).

Plans were initially drawn up to build new large workshops at Wolverhampton but this fell through owing to problems with land acquisition and so expansion at Swindon became the goal. The great new 'A' shops was built between 1901 and 1903 and until that was fully operational, Churchwards plans could only proceed slowly. From 1897, as previously noted, he took a great deal of the day-to-day burden off William Dean whose health was poor and who was ageing rapidly.

For the first of the new express passenger services a large 4-4-0 was designed using 6ft 8½ in driving wheels – this size became the future standard for express passenger locomotives; the first, No. 3292, appeared in December 1897. It was named *Badminton* in April the following year, perhaps as an acknowledgement to the Duke of Beaufort. The new line to South Wales, which left the old line at Wootton Bassett (opened in 1903) would soon see these engines racing towards the Severn Tunnel with dining car expresses, crossing the Duke's Badminton estate. The biggest station on the line was built at Badminton.

The twenty 'Badmintons' were not completed until January 1899 and came between two further batches of 'Dukes' with which they shared some common features including a visual impression devoid of the beauty of the Dean 'singles'. They were however, strong and fast and during this period experimentation on the part of Churchward was mainly confined to boilers.

He wanted boilers that could steam continuously at high rates without water being drawn into the cylinders (priming) and without an unacceptable increase in maintenance. Dry steam and plenty of it was needed and a number of experimental boilers was fitted to various individual 4-4-0s when built. It is not necessary to go into full details here but an important solitary locomotive was built in October 1899, No. 3352 *Camel*. Fundamentally a 'Duke' chassis, the boiler had a large raised, Belpaire firebox and a domeless, parallel boiler barrel while the extended smokebox was completely circular ('drumhead') and rested on, and was fixed to a saddle. Steam was collected in the top front corners of the steam space and the regulator, normally in the dome was moved to the smokebox which in this case was much easier to keep air-tight than the built-up variety.

All the double-frames up to now had been curved but for future 4-4-0s, a new design of straight-top frame was built for increased strength. There were further 'Camels' (later more familiar as the 'Bulldog' class) and the successors to the 'Badmintons' appeared with straight frames and 'Camel' boilers. These were the 'Atbaras', 40 of which were built in 1900-1. A further ten 'Atbaras' were ordered in 1902 but whilst materials were being ordered, one of the earlier 'Atbaras', No. 3405 *Mauritius,* was fitted with a new form of boiler which had a tapered section in the barrel and which also featured some taper rearwards to the firebox sides and top.

Inside the main display at the Great Western Museum Swindon. In view are Lord of the Isle's *driving wheels, the reconstruction of* North Star*, 94XX pannier tank No. 9400, Dean Goods No. 2516 and* City of Truro*.* Lode Star *is out of view.*

(British Railways)

Experiments undertaken in Swindon Works revealed that the circulation of water in a boiler could be affected simply by the method of firing adopted by the firemen with, occasionally, detrimental effects on steaming. This new arrangement, although more difficult to manufacture, eliminated variations in the circulation and made performance more predictable at high rates of working. To manufacture the curved plates involved, new machine tools were purchased.

The importance of the new boiler was such that it caused a complete change in direction from the other experimental boilers and from that time forward all large (and some fairly small) Great Western boilers were of that form. It was taken to the LMSR in 1932 and became standard there and from nationalisation in 1948 standard on BR too.

Surprisingly the boiler fitted to *Mauritius* was not a one-off but one of an order for twenty to be fitted to a new batch of 'Aberdare' 2-6-0 goods engines which had up until that time been turned out with boilers of the 'Camel' type.

Long-term future plans for standardised, large GWR motive power were drawn up in 1901 and included a range of types (4-6-0, 2-8-0, 4-4-0, 2-6-2T and 4-4-2T) all with two outside cylinders, large piston valves and boilers of the 'Camel' form but of larger diameter. Many parts were to be interchangeable between the various types and there was a great deal of American influence in the basic layout.

Only one locomotive actually appeared as envisaged in the original scheme. That was a large 4-6-0, No. 100,

which was completed in February 1902. When George Churchward succeeded William Dean in June 1902 it was fitting that No. 100 was quickly named *Dean* (changed to *William Dean* in November of that year).

A short version of the boiler on No. 100, proposed for the 4-4-0 and the tank engine schemes, was built as a one-off and fitted to 'Aberdare' No. 2661 when new in September 1902, the first of a batch of twenty engines. Twenty of the new tapered standard No. 4 were built for this batch and the one left over was put on the 'Atbara' No. 3405 *Mauritius* (originally built in September 1901), thus producing the prototype 'City'. It is quite possible that the solo boiler put on No. 2661 was originally meant for fitting to an 'Atbara' as an experiment but that step in the development chain was omitted to push things forward.

Although this type of boiler was new to Britain it had been used for ten years in the USA on numerous locomotives built by the Brooks Locomotive Works of Dunkirk, New York. A patent was taken out for some features of the boiler as originally designed in America, under the name of John Player. He was the British-born chief designer at Brooks and many features of his progressive design philosophy were adopted by Churchward in his standard designs.

This type of boiler first made an appearance at the World's Columbian Exposition of 1893 held at Chicago and, in an extensive display of its products, featured on seven of Brooks' locomotives on display. The Great Western Railway had a stand at Chicago (where two surviving broad gauge engines were displayed – *North*

Star and *Lord of the Isles*) and the man in charge, Benjamin J. Hale – who also doubled as the company's PRO man – was chargeman erector at Swindon locomotive works. Off-duty he was a close friend of Churchward's and may well have fed him with brochures and information of Brooks' products.

Another friend of Churchward's was Frederick Harvey Trevithick (grandson of the great Richard), an ex-Swindon man who was CME of the Egyptian State Railways. He visited Canada and the USA in 1900 and in the following year had a 4-6-0 (convertible to a 4-4-2) and a 2-8-0 delivered from Brooks. Both locomotives had the distinctive Player-Belpaire boiler and Churchward may have learned of the good points of the type initially from that source.

MODERNISATION AND NON-STOP TRAINS

One of the reasons for the GWR's need to modernise in the 1890s was the threat of new, competing lines and many of the schemes for new and improved routes by the Great Western were a reaction against such threats. Coal and steel interests in South Wales for example, promoted a 163-mile-long London & South Wales Railway and accommodation with the GWR was reached only when the latter agreed to build the Badminton line (formally, the South Wales and Bristol Direct Railway). It was authorised by Act of Parliament on 7th August 1896 and opened throughout on 1st July 1903.

The Severn Tunnel was something of a bottleneck with regard to coal trains. Many trains were double-headed and also banked from the rear through the tunnel. Train speeds were inevitably low because of the lack of continuous brakes but journey times were lengthened further because of delays in yards for remarshalling and changing engines before negotiating the city of Bristol. Coal traffic could (and did) react on passenger trains and their punctuality.

New lines, freight yards and by-pass loops eventually addressed the problem in association with Churchward's large 2-8-0 design; the 'Aberdare' 2-6-0 was a useful stop-gap and, as things turned out, lasted much longer than expected. (Twelve were nationalised and became 4F; No. 2667 was the last to be withdrawn, in October 1949).

Long before the Badminton line was opened the GWR had introduced a complete new corridor train with a dining car for the South Wales service. Whilst there had been a number of experimental and prototype passenger vehicles built in the early 1890s, it was in 1896 that new standard clerestory designs were built. There were two sets for the ocean liner traffic at Plymouth consisting of eight vehicles each and the South Wales train of six coaches which entered traffic on 11th May 1896. The dining car was first class only, a situation that produced adverse criticism in the press.

One irritant that had to be removed before the GWR could run long-distance non-stop expresses involved the lease to the refreshment rooms at Swindon station. The terms of the lease required every passenger train to stop for at least ten minutes. The lessees were finally bought out in 1895 for what in those days was the enormous sum of £100,000. This appears to have been one of the first major decisions made by the board under the new chairman Viscount Emlyn (later Lord Cawdor). Even before the formal arrangements had been completed, the 'Cornishman' was run non-stop between Paddington and Bristol, 118$\frac{1}{2}$ miles in 2$\frac{1}{4}$ hours – the first non-stop run exceeding 100 miles to have been undertaken on the GWR.

Very quickly some South Wales expresses were being run non-stop to Newport (143$\frac{1}{2}$ miles) and from July 1896 the first portion of the down 'Cornishman' was run non-stop to Exeter (194 miles); this became the longest non-stop run in the country (and possibly, the world).

To run these trains water troughs were laid, firstly at Basildon between Pangbourne and Goring (1895) and at Fox's Wood near Keynsham (1899). More were installed on all the main lines over the next few years including some on the new routes and cut-off lines. In order to run long distances non-stop a new sight-feed lubricator, mounted in the cab, was fitted to the locomotives. This could be controlled and filled by the driver whilst running. Previously the lubricators – and we are interested in cylinders, valves and the regulator here – were filled before the start of a journey and adjusted to last at least until the first stop. Occasionally the driver would have to clamber along the footplate and do some oiling on the move. At high speeds this became unacceptable. It was during this period that passenger deaths per million miles travelled by train had fallen to a very low figure (because of the 1889 Act of Parliament which forced railway companies to adopt continuous automatic brakes on passenger trains and required that the lines on which such trains ran must be controlled by the absolute block system of signalling); deaths of railway workers, however, were increasing and had become a matter for political debate.

The first exceptional non-stop runs on the West Country route were not ocean liner specials nor were they test trains. They were, in fact, *Royal* specials.

On 7th March 1902 the King and Queen travelled from Paddington to Kingswear (via Bristol) non-stop: 228$\frac{1}{2}$ miles in 4 hours 22$\frac{1}{2}$ minutes. The purpose of the journey was to lay the foundation stone of the Royal Naval College at Dartmouth and the return was made on 10th March from Plymouth Millbay to Paddington non-

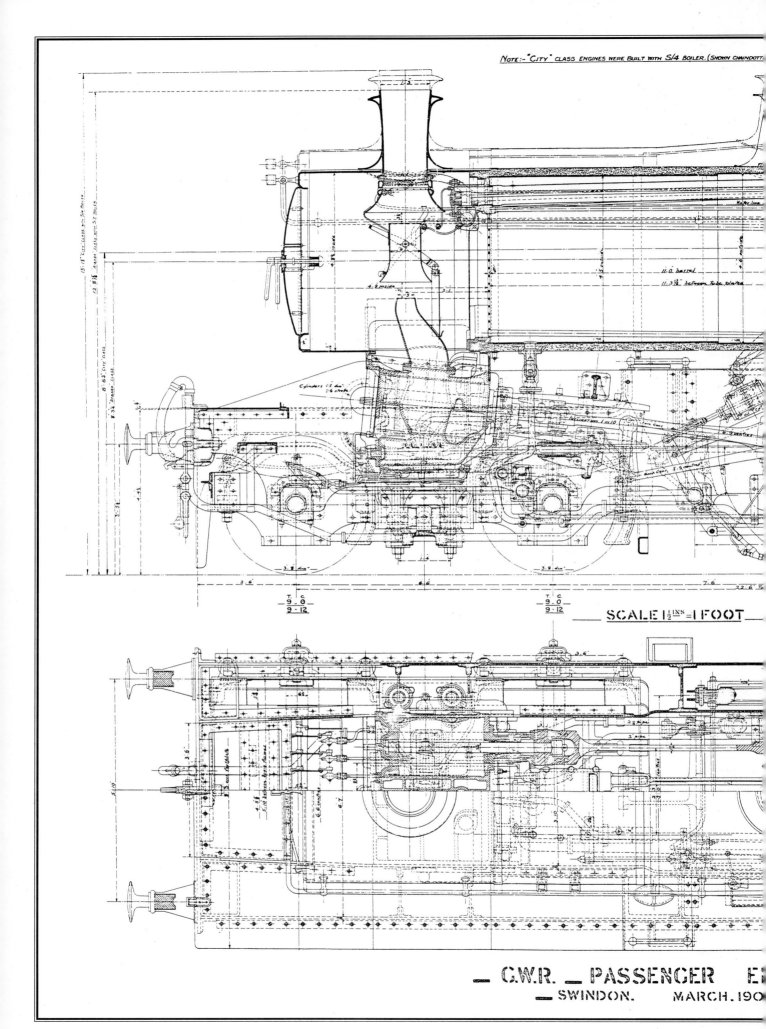

NOTE:- "CITY" CLASS ENGINES WERE BUILT WITH S/4 BOILER. (SHOWN CHAINDOTT.

SCALE 1½ INS = 1 FOOT

G.W.R. _ PASSENGER E

SWINDON.   MARCH. 190

20

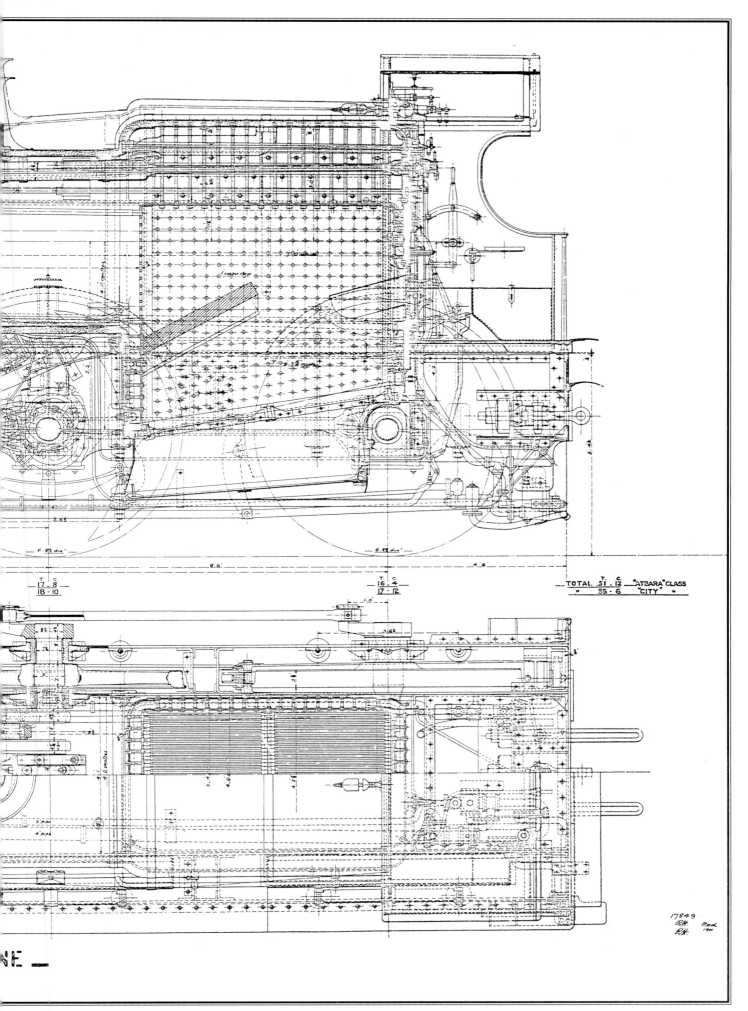

TOTAL. 51 · 12 "ATBARA" CLASS
" 55 · 6 "CITY" "

City of Truro *at Newbury with*
a DN&S line train
(J.S. Gilks collection)

stop: 246½ miles in 4 hours and 44 minutes. The down journey was over twenty minutes inside the booked time and the two runs were the longest non-stop runs attempted by the GWR up to that time. No high speeds were achieved or attempted but the whole operation was carried out well. There were – then – many severe speed restrictions in force and a stretch of single line along the coastal section in south Devon but the working gave notice of what the company was planning. It should also be added that the special arrangements involved when Queen Victoria was travelling – a pilot engine running a block ahead – had been discontinued. The locomotive used was 'Atbara' class 4-4-0 No. 3374 *Baden Powell* having been temporarily renamed for the occasion *Britannia* and the driver on both occasions was Ted Burden of Westbourne Park shed (the name of his fireman is not recorded).

The same driver was entrusted with an even more spectacular 'bash' a year later on 14th July 1903. That train, made up of three Royal vehicles and two ordinary firsts, carried the Prince and Princess of Wales (later King George V and Queen Mary) non-stop from Paddington to Plymouth (via the Bristol avoiding line). The train was run in the path prepared for an advanced portion of the 'Cornishman' and was headed by 4-4-0 No. 3433 *City of Bath*. Built in March that year, No. 3433 was the first of the production 'Cities', the other nine being completed in May.

His Royal Highness had apparently indicated that he would like 'a good run' and this is indeed what he got. The first 194 miles to Exeter were run at an average speed of 67.3 mph but the absolute maximum was only 87½ mph down Dauntsey bank. Despite the difficulties and restrictions of the South Devon line the overall average from Paddington to Plymouth North Road was

63.2 mph 245½ miles in 233½ minutes. Ted Burden and his unknown fireman had knocked 37 minutes off the schedule and set a record that stood for many, many years. It was one of the peaks of footplate work before the days of big, superheated engines but more importantly the whole trip had been done in a very safe manner – high-speed cruising for the most part – none of the 'hot-rod' white-knuckle stuff experienced on occasions during the 'Races to the North' in 1895! From a public (and therefore safety) point of view it had been a *Royal* train and it was unthinkable that any railway authority would put the future King's life at risk. Thus when the company introduced fast, long-distance non-stop trains – with full dining facilities – for those in a position to pay (particularly ocean liner passengers) the service would not be regarded as in any way novel, just the best.

The most direct result was the inauguration of a new express service on 1st July 1904 – 'The Riviera Express' (the name was selected from a competition held by the *Railway Magazine*) – which was worked non-stop between Paddington and Plymouth. By the time of its introduction, several of Churchward's big 4-6-0s were in traffic as was the French de Glehn compound 4-4-2 No. 102 *La France*. The latter in fact worked the very first down non-stop but the service was indiscriminately shared between the big new engines and 'City' and 'Atbara' 4-4-0s.

The publicity surrounding the new non-stop train, better known later as the 'Cornish Riviera Express' or the '10.30 Limited', was preceded by several weeks of 'Ocean Mails' racing trains culminating in *City of Truro's* record run on 9th May. On reflection it does look as though those weeks of racing were meant to give the GWR plenty of publicity in time for the new services.

OCEAN LINERS AND FOREIGN MAILS

Of all the misunderstandings regarding the record run of *City of Truro* – and the publicised record at the time was for the overall running from Plymouth to London – that concerning the connections made with ocean liners at Plymouth, the carrying of international mails and competition between the GWR and the London & South Western Railway is of fundamental importance. It may well be worthwhile, therefore, to take a brief look at the history of this traffic.

Not only had Isambard Kingdom Brunel been the engineer of the original broad gauge Great Western Railway and its associated connecting lines to the west but he was a pioneer of ocean-going steamships and his PS *Great Western* of 1838 (owned by the Great Western Steam Ship Company, formed in 1836) was intended to extend the GWR main line from Paddington to Bristol onward to New York. Competing lines and ships were quickly organised and designed.

There was a need for faster Atlantic crossings and many merchants (and passengers) were prepared to pay for speedier and more predictable timings. An attempt had been made in this direction as early as 1816 when the Black Ball Line of the USA began running regular fast sailing clippers on the North Atlantic run. Whether full or empty, in fine weather or bad, one of the company packets left New York pier bound for Liverpool on the first of every month. Nevertheless Atlantic crossings were always at the mercy of the winds and their direction.

For example, in 1839 westward-bound packet liners averaged 34 days 1¼ hours between Liverpool and New York but the fastest was 22 days and the longest 48 days. Sailing ships, in order to find favourable winds, had

often to travel considerably longer distances than a more direct steamer would. Eastward-bound figures for the same year were 22 days 1 hour on average, 17 days for the fastest and 36 days for the slowest.

The good burghers of Bristol did not have the foresight of their main competitors in Liverpool. In the latter city, the docks were expanded, steam tugs were used from the earliest days and charges were much less. The Great Western Steam Ship Co. moved base to the northern port in 1842 despite the *Great Western* having already demonstrated best times of 13 days 12 hours westbound and 12 days 10 hours eastbound (to and from Bristol). Thus Liverpool became the main port for most of the steamship companies involved in the North Atlantic trade (invariably British-owned and sailing British-built ships) for over 40 years.

There was of course a great deal more trade than this; the port of London was *the* port of the British Empire and there was a complex of routes between many British ports and all corners of the earth, protected by the Royal Navy.

In the days of sail vessels heading south or west via the English Channel usually made Falmouth the final British port of call and the first stop for returning ships. It became a 'packet' port in 1689 with a service to Corunna. (Other packet ports of the seventeenth century were London, Harwich, Dover, Holyhead and Milford).

Traditionally, mail had been sent by way of the shipmaster's mailbag which was hung from a hook in a popular dockside tavern until the ship was due to sail. As trade grew and the Empire expanded this was clearly unsatisfactory and special packet boats were hired on contract by the Post Office. Not only did they carry mail

Following City of Truro's *move to York in August 1986 a test run to Scarborough was undertaken on Wednesday 6th of that month in preparation for working the 'Scarborough Spa Express'. This photograph shows the train making a brief stop at Malton on the outward journey.* (Author)

and packets but were a reliable way to transfer merchants' payments or 'specie' – silver and gold coins.

To return to Falmouth, the first London-Falmouth mail coach service began in 1785 and the port was the base for 35 packet boats. They were fast ships protected by their complement of eighteen guns and crewed by 18 to 40 men who were immune from the predations of Royal Navy press gangs. Contracts were usually for seven years and costs were high. At the beginning of the nineteenth century the charge for sending a letter to America was 3s 7d.(c.18p).

The first cross-Channel steam packet began in 1816 when there was already a number of regular steamboat services in home waters. During the 1820s many more routes were opened and new ships built. Many of the crowds who made their way to attend the opening of the Liverpool & Manchester Railway in 1830 had travelled by a form of steam-powered transport already well-established.

The great advantage of the steamship was that it was not dependent on the wind and therefore timetables could be planned and schedules relied on. Such benefits were overwhelming for mail carriers and passengers while the latter had already begun to provide enough paying customers for pleasure cruises in estuaries and to coastal resorts.

For cargo-carrying there were many disadvantages to the steamship; first cost was very high and cargo space was severely reduced by that taken up by engine, boiler and (especially) coal bunkers. It was also completely dependent on working between suitably placed coaling stations. There was a fear of fire (justifiable when ships were still mostly made of wood) and also of explosions (not seriously likely as the early ships used very low boiler pressures – hence their low thermal efficiency).

Nevertheless British industry, inventors and entrepreneurs in both England and Scotland, almost alone amongst the nations of the world, continued to develop steam for those purposes for which it was most suited at the time.

In 1837, the year of Queen Victoria's accession to the throne, one James MacQueen, critical of existing packet services sent a polemical report to the Government which included a "General Plan for Mail Communication between Great Britain and the Eastern and Western Parts of the World; also to Canton and Sydney westward to the Pacific". He declared, "Steamboats carrying mails should be the mail coaches of the ocean".

It was during this period that the Post Office began awarding contracts to steamship lines backed up by generous government subsidies and it was such backing that enabled companies like Cunard and the Royal Mail Line to establish themselves on the North Atlantic run. The coming of the railways extended the system on land and was a further incentive to speed and efficiency. Rowland Hill's Penny Post of 1840 revolutionised this whole form of communication and brought it within the pocket of almost everyone.

The GWR main line to Bristol was opened on 30th June 1841; the broad gauge was extended to Exeter over the Bristol & Exeter Railway on 1st May 1844 and from Exeter to Plymouth along the line of the South Devon Railway on 2nd April 1849. The SDR terminus was at Millbay. A further extension from Cornwall Junction outside Plymouth was the Cornwall Railway which crossed Brunel's famous Royal Albert Bridge and initially terminated at Truro (opened throughout on 4th May 1859). It was not extended to Falmouth until 1st August 1863 and by that time important ocean liner traffic had moved to Plymouth.

Plymouth Sound and the area around the Saltash

estuary had sustained docks and harbours for many centuries. A new dock at Millbay was authorised by Act of Parliament on 18th August 1846. The engineer appointed was Isambard Brunel and it will come as no surprise to learn that the company was known as the Great Western Dock Co. although it had no financial or organisational links with the GWR at that time. However, within two years, extensions had been authorised and the new capital was subscribed by the three broad gauge railway companies to the east. (They jointly took over the dock company in 1874).

The full complex was opened in June 1857 and from September of that year regular mails by steamer began when the 530 ton *Dane* of the Cape Mail Union Line embarked with passengers and mails bound for Cape Town. In 1867 the Post Office took over control of all overseas mail contracts from the Admiralty and the West Indies mails, formerly carried (and sorted) by packet boats to Falmouth, were transferred to Plymouth Millbay and a broad gauge travelling Post Office introduced from Plymouth to Bristol. One purpose for which Plymouth became very important in the Victorian and Edwardian era was as an emigrant port. Many tens of thousands left, on assisted passages, to make a new life in the colonies.

In January 1882 the Peninsular & Orient Line (P&O) began to use Millbay on a regular basis and for its part the GWR built new facilities directly alongside the quay so that passengers could transfer straight to railway carriages rather than having to make their way on foot or by horse-cab to Millbay terminus, about ¹/3 mile away. Many trains, particular the 'Ocean Mails Specials', began from this new terminal. Typically the train would be in two sections, mail vans on the road along the quayside and passenger carriages on an inner, parallel road with a platform and waiting rooms etc. The passenger section would include plenty of brake vehicles to hold the luggage. If specie was being moved one of the special GWR bullion vans would be allocated. An especially heavy consignment of mails and large numbers of passengers and consequently a great deal of luggage might mean that two trains were run but it was most important that the mails were despatched as quickly as possible. The international telegraph system enabled Plymouth to know exactly how many mailbags and passengers to expect and also whether a bullion van or other special vehicles would be needed.

The mail contracts with the Post Office were lucrative for those railway companies involved but timings were set down in agreement with the Postmaster General and his staff. Schedules and their observation were of the utmost importance and the vehicles used were designed to suit Post Office requirements. All vehicles were allocated to particular services and Post Office trains were marshalled in pre-arranged formations. During the period of intense competition between the lines running the North Atlantic services in the 1890s and after, it was possible that a liner's arrival in Plymouth Sound would be several hours earlier than expected. Trains would be despatched when loaded, however, and a timetable path arranged using the same sectional passing times.

The London & South Western Railway had first arrived in Plymouth over its standard gauge line from Exeter in 1876. Running powers over sections of the GWR resulted in mixed-gauge track being laid and a new joint station constructed at North Road but the latter's construction was paid for by the LSWR. The company had a station on its own line at Devonport and there was a rather inconvenient branch down to Stonehouse Pool Quay which was initially worked (from 1881) as freight-only.

Unlike its eastern neighbours in Kent and Sussex, the LSWR had no packet ports but in November 1892 purchased Southampton Docks and immediately set about improvement and enlargement. The Prince of Wales Graving Dock – the largest in the world – was opened by His Royal Highness on 3rd August 1895. Soon many of the important Continental shipping lines active on the North Atlantic services (such as North German Lloyd, Hamburg-America Line etc) were calling at Southampton.

The 'modern' era of giant fast liners on the service to and from New York really began in 1888 with the *City of New York* and her sister ship *City of Paris* operated by the Liverpool-based Inman Line. The pair had been constructed on the Clyde at the yard of J. and G. Thomson Ltd. They were all-steel, twin-screw vessels fitted with two triple-expansion engines producing 20,100 shaft horsepower per ship enabling speeds of over 20 knots to be achieved. *City of Paris* held the Blue Riband for several years and was the first liner to cross the Atlantic in less than six days.

These were the first liners of over 10,000 GRT (Gross Registered Tons) since Brunel's ill-fated *Great Eastern* of 1858 whose last voyage, ironically, from the Clyde to Birkenhead for breaking up also took place in 1888.

Both ships were purchased by the American Line in 1893 and renamed *New York* and *Paris* respectively. It is said that the sale was due to financial difficulties of the Inman Line but in fact both were part of John Pierpoint Morgan's vast empire. The American Line was originally conceived by the Pennsylvania Railroad in 1873. J.P. Morgan had control of American, Inman and the Belgian Red Star Line by 1886 and the extent of his control continued to grow.

In purchasing the liners, American Line needed the permission of the U.S. Congress and this was given with the proviso that two similar ships should be ordered from American shipbuilding yards. That was agreed and the *St.*

Louis and *St. Paul* were launched from Cramp's Yard, Philadelphia and made maiden voyages in 1895 but there were teething troubles and modifications made to both ships.

Most of the shipping lines operated on one or two days per week in either direction and the Post Office might use different lines outward from Liverpool, while the U.S. Mails would use the other lines to despatch its mails. The American Line eventually gained this contract and moved its British base to Southampton. The LSWR's carriage superintendent William Panter designed special stock for the new passenger service known as the 'American Eagle Express'. The new coaches were fitted with Fox's patent pressed steel bogies and there were two sets both of nine coaches; the trains were completed with a six-wheeled van at either end.

The important Continental lines allowed passengers to disembark along with any mails at Plymouth and Cherbourg before continuing to their home ports – the North German Lloyd to Bremen, Hamburg-America Line to Hamburg and Holland-America Line to Rotterdam. There was no question of these vessels docking at Plymouth; they dropped anchor in Plymouth Sound and two small boats – tenders – which were owned by the GWR moved alongside the liner (one on either side). One took the mail and the other passengers and their luggage.

Things really began to hot up in 1897. The German government, like many in Europe, was anxious to help numerous small farmers, and their families living in peasant-like poverty, to emigrate to the USA, allowing farms at home to be consolidated and made more efficient. Many *were* leaving in the final decades of the nineteenth century but their subsidised fares were going into the pockets of British shipping line owners. In that year the first of a number of massive, powerful and fast liners entered service, encouraged and financed to a great extent by the German government. The ships were intended to compete at all levels of the market including considerable steerage accommodation for emigrants.

The ships in question – all built at the Vulcan yard, Stettin, for North German Lloyd – undertook their maiden voyages as follows: *Kaiser Wilhelm der Grosse* in September 1897; *Kronprinz Wilhelm* in September 1901 and *Kaiser Wilhelm II* in April 1903. Together with another Vulcan ship, the *Deutschland* (maiden voyage July 1900) of the Hamburg-America Line, these remarkable liners seized and held the Blue Riband for Germany from 1897 to 1907, breaking new records year on year.

In June 1907 a final vessel the *Kronprinzessin Cecilie* entered service, having the largest reciprocating engines ever to be installed in a ship (45,000 ihp) but within months it was seen to be obsolete when the two great British Cunarders, *Lusitania* and *Mauritania*, both powered by turbines (of 76,000 and 78,000 hp respectively) entered service. *Lusitania* regained the Blue Riband in October but from September 1909, for over twenty years continuously, it was held by *Mauritania*.

These two giants were Government-backed, subsidised by the Admiralty for conversion to fast cruisers in times of war. J.P. Morgan, who had swallowed up the White Star Line in 1902, had his eyes on the Cunard company too and the British government was as fearful of an American monopoly of the North Atlantic 'Ferry' as it was of the growing German navy.

The White Star Line moved headquarters from Liverpool to Southampton in 1902 (it returned to British ownership in 1927) and was later followed by Cunard (in 1919). Whilst this ended the Great Western Railway's attempt to tap into Liverpool-bound liner traffic (using tenders as at Plymouth) at Fishguard, all lines could now disembark passengers and mails in Plymouth Sound and Ocean Liner specials operated from Millbay Docks to Paddington until 1962.

RACING TRAINS AND RECORDS

Any reader even slightly familiar already with *City of Truro's* exploits and the 'racing trains' of 1904 might be puzzled as to what exactly the fuss was about; there was already an accepted pattern of ship-rail interchange at Plymouth as well as firm contracts between the Post Office and the GWR regarding TPOs and 'Special Mails'.

The 'racing' only involved the liners of the American Line everything else was 'spin' by Paddington's publicity section (then called the Advertising Department) which was given a major boost in January 1904 when the Chief Engineer, James C. Inglis, was appointed general manager following the death of Sir Joseph Wilkinson. Early in the year the company's first book was published, a handsome volume of 152 pages entitled *The Cornish Riviera*; fully illustrated and including maps it was priced at 3d. (1¼ new pence). That a new express was planned for the summer timetable beginning in July (later to be named 'The Cornish Riviera Limited') and running non-stop from Paddington to Plymouth leaves us in no doubt as to what all the publicity was really about.

In 1903 the American Line announced that eastbound trans-Atlantic sailings would call at Plymouth. The LSWR, in collaboration rented more land at Stonehouse Pool quay and built a passenger terminal with all facilities. An attempt to obtain a mail contract with the GPO was rebuffed; the GWR TPO carried a Bristol portion which was detached at Bristol and then coupled to the North and Midlands mails whereas the LSWR's route did not allow for such a straightforward (and established) connection.

The first vessel to call was the *St. Louis* on 9th April 1904. It has since been stated that there was 'an agreement' between the GWR (mails) and the LSWR (passengers) but this is untrue. We have seen that the mails were the GWR's anyway. Passengers disembarking from the *St. Louis* were refused access to a GWR tender and were forced to go to Stonehouse pool. Those who then hired cabs to Millbay – almost certainly those wanting connections by train to the Midlands, South Wales, the North etc. – found the Great Western train had long since departed. The train journey from Southampton to Waterloo was 'free' in that it was included in the liner fare but is not clear if the Stonehouse Pool to Waterloo fare was also free. The trains were worked into Devonport (Kings Road) but although locomotives were changed at Templecombe there were no official stops.

The *Great Western Magazine* was originally published

in 1888 by the GWR Temperance Union. It was a worthy if rather bland bulletin and by 1903 had a circulation of only 2,500 and the Temperance Union was in financial trouble. The company cleared the Union's debts (these were mainly concerned with Coffee Taverns) and in August that year Felix Pole, a junior in the general manager's office, took over as editor, a task he performed in his spare time! In early 1904 he obtained the services of A. J. L. White of the CME's department at Swindon and began publishing lists of engine names and numbers and making the magazine more available to the general public. By May 1904 circulation had shot up to 11,000 and there is no doubt that topical articles and comment spiced up the journal considerably.

With regard to the first American Line arrival at Plymouth, after stating that the existing GWR arrangements at Millbay "have left nothing to be desired" the US shipping company came in for some criticism: "Some of the passengers wished to land with the mails and use the Millbay Station services at Plymouth but were not allowed to and were compelled to go to Stonehouse Pool where they were forced to pay landing dues which would not have been chargeable at Millbay". The writer went on, "The Great Western Company are always ready to meet fair and legitimate competition but it is difficult to understand the attitude adopted by the American Line".

The result was related with some satisfaction in that the mails, of approximately 1,200 bags, "Notwithstanding the labour involved [were loaded and the GWR] managed to get their special train into Paddington 18 minutes before the South Western train conveying passengers reached Waterloo". The GW route to London was eighteen miles longer too and on this occasion engines were changed twice, at Exeter and at Bristol.

The *St. Louis* had arrived four hours before its expected time of c. 6.00am. The information that an early arrival was on the cards was probably learned via a radio link – the sister ship the *St. Paul* was the first vessel to use Marconi's apparatus for ship-to-shore communication, in 1897. The LSWR managed to get all the staff out of bed and on the job by 1.30am; many senior officers were on duty including Henry Holmes, the Superintendent of the Line and the formidable Locomotive Superin-tendent Dugald Drummond. 57 passengers and their luggage transferred to the LSWR tender at around 3.30am, the train departing at 5.03am. At such a time and with so many passengers, the GWR would have no doubt produced the option of a sleeping car but the LSWR did not own any.

For the LSWR's publicity G. A. Sekon, founder and editor of the *Railway Magazine*, was invited to travel and write up his experiences. The GWR invited the Rev. W.J. Scott, an inveterate and experienced train-timer, to travel with the mails. Such events were reported in detail in newspapers as well as magazines in those days; there was much public interest in modern fast transport both on sea and rail. The American Line called at Plymouth once a week only; the two German Lines also called once each per week and their mails and passengers were purely a GWR affair as mostly were ships from Australia, India, South Africa etc. which also called regularly.

Over the next four weeks a number of the trans-Atlantic arrivals were met by GWR staff who were exceptionally well-prepared and quickly despatched fast mail specials. Even with the normal German lines' connections, the mails were sent separately from any passengers. These preparations were more than just a swipe at the LSWR but were in association with the liners' attempts to make new records for steaming across the Atlantic and thus a record time in taking the mails from New York to London. There is no doubt that the American Line was attempting to grab the Blue Riband from North German Lloyd but the German ships were the best of the day.

The South Western had a brief moment of glory on Saturday 23rd April when the passenger special ran from Stonehouse Junction to Waterloo in 4 hours 3 minutes against 4 hours 12 minutes for the GWR's mail special. That record was short-lived, however; a week late the Great Western had reduced its time to 3 hours 54 minutes and was geared up for some sort of spectacular finale.

This came on 9th May. It had been meticulously planned and of course experience had been gained by footplate crews, signalmen and train guards and the knowledge circulated amongst their peers.

The Times of Thursday 5th May 1904 reported that the *Kronprinz Wilhelm* had left New York at 10.00am (local time?) on 3rd bound for Plymouth, Cherbourg and Bremen. It reported that $1.5 million in gold bullion was being carried, as part payment by the U.S. Government to the French one, for the Panama Canal. It has since been stated many times that the gold was taken off the ship at Plymouth and travelled by the Ocean Mails Special. This, however, was one of official train timer, Charles Rous-Marten's, many errors. The gold went on to Cherbourg and was unloaded on to French soil (obviously, surely?). No such shipment could have been put on a tender and unloaded again and carried once more to the train at Millbay quay. Such a consignment, worth perhaps a hundred times as much today would have weighed several

City of Truro *in the area of the NRM formerly known as the 'dutch barn', in steam and ready to go. The shade of red applied to the frames is more subdued (and the correct one) than that applied in 1957.*

(Author)

In York station waiting to depart with the 'Scarborough Spa Express in the summer of 1987.

(Author)

On the turntable at Scarborough. This equipment had been recovered from Gateshead depot and was built by Cowan & Sheldon of Carlisle in 1909 – nearly as old as City of Truro! *Note the pressed steel sleepers on the track in the left foreground.* (Author)

City of Truro *with a down SSE at Weaverthorpe in August 1988.*

(T.J. Edgington)

City of Truro *at Nottingham (Midland) on a cold and wet morning after running with the support coach from York via Sheffield and the Erewash Valley line (the line into Derby from the north was in the possession of the civil engineer). After running round and then turning at Trent 3440 was facing the right way to take a SLOA excursion from Derby to Didcot. Unfortunately it developed a hot tender axlebox after Birmingham and had to be taken off the train.*

(Author)

Engine and support coach en route for Butterley were photographed at Royd Moor near Frickley on the Swinton & Knottingley Joint line.

(J.S. Gilks)

In the 'dutch barn' at the NRM No. 3440 stands next to LNER V2 class No. 4771 Green Arrow, *which is being prepared for a 'Scarborough Spa Express' duty.* (Author)

A view from underneath City of Truro *taken from an inspection pit looking towards the front of the engine. The large cast motion bracket-cum-frame stretcher can be seen. This supports the outer ends of the slidebars. The eccentrics and their rods are in the centre (upper) and the inner crank webs can just be discerned at the left and right.*

(Author)

In 1989 City of Truro *visited Utrecht in Holland, the headquarters and hub of the railway network for NS 150. The motive power depot was temporarily adapted to deal with steam locomotives from many countries in Europe. No. 3440 can be seen in the company of Swiss four-cylinder compound 2-10-0 No. 2910.*

(Author)

The cavalcade loco-motives at Utrecht, coupled together begin to make their way, in reverse, back to the depot. City of Truro *is sandwiched between a diminutive fireless locomotive and an East German class 03 Pacific.*

(Author)

City of Truro *makes a runpast during the cavalcades with Richard Gibbon and Jane Elliott of the NRM in charge.*

(Author)

City of Truro *back safely in York after her Ambassadorial role with the staff who took turns to look after her in Utrecht. Standing L-R: Tony Hall-Patch (Science Museum), Richard Gibbon, Helen Ashby, John Smith, Beverley Cole, Jane Elliott, Ray Towell; On footplate L-R: Mike Rutherford, Mike Blakemore, Dave Burrows.*

(NRM)

tons and would have taken most of the morning to tranship as well as requiring extensive security. It would also have been put into a specialised bullion van and attached to the passenger train, *not* the Post Office train.

Kronprinz Wilhelm arrived in Plymouth Sound on Monday 9th May at 8.00am and both mail (c.1,300 bags) and passengers with their luggage were transferred to the tender *Cheshire* (the vessel's first ever duty). The tender docked at about 8.30 and while the passengers and their luggage negotiated customs, the mails were quickly loaded into the five-van Ocean Mails Special, the first three vehicles for Paddington and the rear two, with the portion of mails for the Midlands and the North, to be detached on the Bristol avoiding line at Pylle Hill.

The mails were flagged away at 9.19am for the short run to Millbay Crossing where the tank engine used in the dock area was replaced by No. 3440 *City of Truro* and set off with a determined Moses Clements of Exeter shed at the regulator, at 8.23am. It is believed that the fireman was one William Bickley who was employed as Outside Foreman at Laira locomotive depot during World War II.

There is no doubt that the GWR was intent on producing a run to Paddington that would be beyond the LSWR to emulate. The Assistant Superintendent of the Line, Charles Aldington was in attendance and Charles Rous-Marten had been invited to time the train on this occasion. Timings had become of great interest to the public and an independent observer was regarded as a better bet than publishing no more than the guard's log.

Details were not only published in the technical and railway press but also in the newspapers. People like Rous-Marten were often in demand as expert pundits. He was a New Zealander and something of a self-appointed expert on locomotive performance. He wrote regularly in the *Engineer* and *Railway Magazine* and began the long-running series in the latter magazine "British Locomotive Practice and Performance" which, under a slightly different title is produced monthly to this day. Some have claimed that his work was as accurate and meticulous as was possible; others have been of a different opinion. The late Geoffrey Freeman Allen quoted a letter his father (Cecil J. Allen, the doyen of all timers) possessed from a Rous-Marten contemporary who said that the New Zealander did not check his quarter-mile speed timings against his station-to-station times, was prone to rounding down his quarter-mile times and was not careful to keep a constant viewing angle when looking out for quarter-mile posts. At high speeds these idiosyncrasies could lead to dubious speed calculations. (Freeman Allen thought that the critic was R.E. Charlewood, a railway employee and a timer at least as experienced as Rous-Marten).

Certainly with regard to events on 9th May 1904 Rous-Marten made a number of errors. We started with the gold bullion but he also estimated the train weight incorrectly, claiming 148 tons gross when in fact it was about 30 tons less. It is thought that the tare weights were not marked on GW vehicles at that time. He may have asked the guard or a post office employee and been given

the gross weight, thought it was tare and added the estimated load again.

It seems likely that he caught the train by the skin of his teeth, possible boarding at the brief stop at Millbay Crossing which is near Millbay Station. He would no doubt have travelled down overnight (which was a Sunday) and, with the *Kronprinz Wilhelm* arriving early, have perhaps misjudged things, trying to get a breakfast at Millbay perhaps (the Sunday night sleeping car was put on the 10.00pm ex-Paddington due in Millbay at 4.53am Monday morning in 1902; times may have changed by 1904).

Rous-Marten's log was published on 10th May in the *Western Daily Mercury* and the *Western Morning News*. It is almost certain that it was telephoned from Paddington (there weren't many telephones around in those days). Exactly the same log appeared in the *Railway Magazine* and elsewhere under the name of Rous-Marten but intermediate maximum speeds were not given. The newspaper reports in the west had much more information, however, not only plenty of factual detail regarding the number of mailbags and load etc but the *Mercury* report also said, "five minutes were occupied between Wellington and Taunton … the speed being terrific and at times being between ninety-nine and a hundred miles an hour …".

This additional information came from a Mr. William Kennedy, one of the Post Office letter-sorters on duty on the train. He had used a stopwatch but by the time his identity was ascertained he was deceased and no log survived.

Rous-Marten must have notified Charles Aldington of the maximum speed (according to him) of 102.3 mph and been told to keep it under his hat. The following year he wrote to James Inglis, the GWR General Manager with a plea to publish full details and in his letter included a number of quarter-mile times from leaving Whitehall tunnel and accelerating down the bank. Once again the GW authorities did not wish for the details to be published (although Rous-Marten cryptically referred to having travelled at 102.3 mph on one occasion) but the month before he died, in answer to a reader's query revealed the speed and the occasion (*Railway Magazine* April 1908 issue) in detail. This appears to have been overlooked ever since. He died in 1908 and Inglis followed in 1911, after which the whole matter was forgotten until November 1922 when the Rous-Marten letter was published in the November issue of the *Great Western Railway Magazine* – very handy for publicity at the hour of the grouping! *Railway Magazine* obliged in its December issue by claiming that the details had been common knowledge to the cognoscenti for many years.

Things went quiet again fortunately long enough for the engine to have been preserved and tucked away in York Museum in 1931. Three years later it became a *cause célèbre* in the "British Locomotive Practice and Performance" articles, then penned by C.J. Allen and many analyses were carried out and reconstructions of 'how it might have been' were formulated. Controversy was heightened because of the growing speed exploits of Nigel Gresley's Pacifics on the LNER and particularly the running of No. 4472 *Flying Scotsman* on 30th November 1934 when 100 mph was observed in the dynamometer car. This claimed the attention of LNER supporters who recognised this as the first official 100 mph by steam, in Britain at least. Although some saw it as a 'world record', the Pennsylvania Railroad had achieved 'the ton' over a mile, during high-speed tests in 1908 when an Atlantic and a lone test car were used to test new steel bridges for hammer-blow (deflection

A shot taken in evening sunshine of City of Truro *coupled to the magnificently restored clerestory non-corridor third class carriage at the Great Western Society's base at Didcot Railway Centre.* (Author)

meters etc were fitted to the bridges) on that railroad's racetrack – the Fort Wayne Division.

The GWR vs LNER debate has festered ever since (it started, of course, with the 1925 interchange trials in which the Gresley Pacifics came off second best). Any editor short of copy has found it easy to stir things up by baiting either GWR supporters or Gresley fans – and the sport continues!

To repeat, however, *City of Truro's* record of the 9th May 1904 was in its running from Plymouth to Bristol and we should not forget the second leg, on to Paddington, by the Dean 4-2-2 No. 3065 *Duke of Connaught* when the 118.7 miles from Pylle Hill Junction to Paddington were run in 99 minutes and 46 seconds. There is reason to believe that No. 3440 was expected to undertake the whole journey solo but the remaining coal in the tender at Bristol might have been problematic and so the single, standing by in any case, was put on.

DULL DUTIES AND DELIVERANCE

The 'City' performances were outstanding in their early years; the combination of an excellent free-running chassis and a superbly steaming boiler indicated that there were no workings at that time which they could not handle. In 1904 dynamometer car trials took place to compare the French-built 4-4-2 de Glehn compound No. 102 *La France* and Churchward's two-cylinder 4-6-0 No. 171 *Albion*. These were given plenty of publicity and worked the new non-stop express in July (named 'Cornish Riviera Limited' in 1905) turn about with 'Cities' and even 'Atbaras'. The 1904 train consisted of a five-coach clerestory set, a 70ft 'Dreadnought' dining car and a tri-composite through coach for Falmouth. When named in the following summer, seven of the new 'Dreadnought' design were used.

Churchward's larger new standard engines could not be produced fast enough and new sheds with large turntables constructed quickly enough to keep up with demands. Seventeen of the earlier 'Badmintons' were therefore rebuilt with the standard No. 4 ('City') boiler between November 1903 and March 1910 and a further nine 'Atbaras' so treated between February 1907 and February 1909. The latter remained as 'Cities' for the rest of their lives but the 'Badmintons' were fitted with the smaller standard No. 2 in 1911-13 when their use on main line work was no longer required.

Once all the new cut-off lines were open and new sheds and other facilities in business, the 'Cities' gradually moved away from the west of England main line and to the South Wales and Birmingham routes. *City of Truro* was allocated to sheds in the west until July 1923 (the 'Castles' were introduced that August) when it was transferred to Wolverhampton and remained in the Northern Division until final withdrawal in March 1931, following which it was presented to the Railway Museum, York. It had run 1,000,669 miles and a residual value of £235 was put on it.

At the time of its withdrawal there was little left of the engine as built except the frames. Boilers and tenders were exchanged during heavy repairs at Swindon Works while many original design features were discontinued and replaced by later practices.

The cylinder block had been replaced by one with piston valves, the steam reverser had been replaced by the screw type, the bogie had been modified to accommodate 'spittoon' side bearers and all boilers fitted after September 1911 had superheaters and the top-feed arrangement of clacks. The plain blastpipe and petticoat had been replaced with a jumper-top blastpipe and no petticoat. The 1912 number – 3717 – was retained.

It is unlikely that in its later condition *City of Truro* could have reached 100 mph whereas when built it certainly had the potential. The engine's final work included Chester to Oxford, Oxford to London and Shrewsbury to Bristol trains. It left Swindon on 20th March at 3.30 am and was hauled dead, as part of a goods train, to Banbury where it was handed over to the LNER. On arrival in York, E.M. Bywell, the Curator of the Railway Museum arranged a photo shoot in the old station and *City of Truro* was pictured alongside A1 Pacific No. 2572 *St. Gatien* which was, "fresh off the 'Flying Scotsman'".

Apart from a period of evacuation to Sprouston, near Kelso, during the Second World War, No. 3717 remained at York until 9th January 1957 when it was, "on loan to the Western Region from York Museum" and was removed to Swindon for restoration to running order. The boiler was changed and Automatic Train Control (ATC) equipment fitted. The livery applied was claimed to be that of 1903 but there were many criticisms, not least the shade of red applied to the outside frames. Nevertheless No. 3440 (renumbered back from 3717 so as not to cause confusion with the pannier tank carrying the same number) was a fine sight and was one more manifestation of the freedom that the B R Regions had enjoyed since the end of the Railway Executive in 1953. The Western Region had reintroduced brown and cream carriage livery for the more important expresses and most were given romantic names evoking the GWR tradition. Many locomotives painted a drab black since nationalisation suddenly emerged from Swindon Works in lined green. This use of tradition was a balance to the modernisation that was beginning; diesel railcars for main lines as well as commuting services were spreading and the first of the high-powered diesel locomotives were being planned and constructed at Swindon alongside new standard steam locomotive construction.

If there had been a precursor to *City of Truro's* restoration it was probably the working of the two 'Plant Centenarian' specials in September 1953 in connection with the centenary of Doncaster Works. The specials were worked by a pair of Great Northern Atlantics, No. 990 *Henry Oakley* and wide firebox variety No. 251, both being the first of their class. No. 990 was a York Museum engine, having been there since January 1938, while No. 251 had just been withdrawn and was kept in Doncaster paint shop after restoration. When *City of Truro* moved

to Swindon in 1957, No. 251 took its place at York.

Having been influenced by those earlier specials, the restoration of No. 3440 also had repercussions, notably on the Scottish Region which restored four engines (two were already museum engines, the other pair became so) and the London Midland Region which restored the 'Crimson Rambler', ex-Midland Railway three-cylinder compound No. 1000. *City of Truro* appeared with most of these engines in exhibitions and double-headed on special trains.

Unique amongst all these other restorations No. 3440 was a traffic machine and filled in between special excursions and exhibitions with revenue-earning duties although ex-London & South Western Railway T9 class 4-4-0 No. 30120 was restored to pre-grouping livery in March 1962 when still in traffic. (Withdrawn in July 1963 this locomotive is also part of the National Collection). This was the plan from the very beginning and after some running in turns from Swindon to Didcot, Bath and Bristol it was allocated to Didcot and worked trains on the Didcot, Newbury & Southampton line – the 12.42 from Didcot to Southampton Terminus and the 4.56 return. During the summer of 1958 No. 3440 worked some commuters' trains – the 7.30 am Reading to Paddington and the 6.20 pm return. When the DN&S was earmarked for closure, *City of Truro* was transferred to Swindon and it was regularly used to haul Engineer's inspection saloons. It also began a regular duty involving Swindon, Bristol (both routes) and Weston-Super-Mare.

Most of September 1959 was spent in Scotland with the other working museum engines, on display as well as working special trains associated with the Scottish Industries Fair.

By 1960 excursions with No. 3440 were fewer and there was less traffic work to do, so *City of Truro* was officially withdrawn from stock in May 1961. It was repainted in a very plain green livery with black frames, numbered 3717 once more and placed in the new Great Western Railway Museum at Swindon in the former Wesleyan Chapel. The Museum was formally opened on 24th June 1962.

After a long and uneventful rest of 22 years *City of Truro* became an important actor in a great pageant being prepared to celebrate the 150th Anniversary of the Act of Parliament of 1835 that authorised the Great Western Railway to raise capital and build a railway from London to Bristol.

It was to be a major event not only with main line specials and activities on relevant preserved lines but Swindon was also to play a major part and that would be centred on the works. The 'Factory' as it was universally known had suffered a good deal over the years through partial closures and redundancies and there had always been the threat of something worse in the background. Even so it came as something of a bolt out of the blue when total closure was announced in the build-up to 'GWR-150'. Inevitably the Swindon events were cancelled but *City of Truro* had already been taken from Swindon Museum to the workshops of the Severn Valley Railway at Bridgnorth. It was not until 3rd September 1985 that it was ready to undertake main line trials but a return run from Kidderminster to Gloucester and back that day was a great success and a 'Mystery Tour' was advertised for 25th October.

There was little 'mystery' about it as every photographer within a couple of hundred miles was waiting for the eight Mk1 coaches and No. 3440 (renumbered yet again!) on the Gloucester to Newport and return working.

Following scheduled working on the SVR in the summer of 1986, interspersed by a couple of main line trips, *City of Truro* was moved to York where it appeared on museum display between turns hauling the 'Scarborough Spa Express'. This state of affairs continued through 1987 to 1989 when in April of that year it was earmarked for the 'Western Adventurer' from Derby to Didcot but had to be removed at Dorridge with a hot tender axlebox. This fault was corrected at Tyseley and the engine worked to Didcot ready to haul an Inter-City VIP Special to Stratford-upon-Avon on 13th May. The following day *City of Truro* worked the demonstration line at the Great Western Railway Society's Didcot site double-headed with the preserved 'Dukedog' No. 3217 *Earl of Berkeley*, the only other surviving double-framed 4-4-0.

In June No. 3440 was taken by road to Sheerness Docks and loaded aboard a ferry to Rotterdam, en route to Utrecht in Holland where it was to appear in the Dutch Railways' 150th Anniversary celebration as Britain's official representative.

This was an extremely successful event and attracted working steam locomotives from many countries in Europe, including France, Germany (both East and West) Czechoslovakia, Poland, Switzerland and Holland. The Dutch National Railway Museum's contribution was a handsome, four-cylinder 4-6-0 to a design of Beyer, Peacock of Manchester. Resplendent in a green livery adorned with much copper and brass, it was clearly a cousin of *City of Truro*.

No. 3440 returned from Rotterdam via the Exxtor Terminal at Immingham and by road back to York for display in the NRM. This visit was to be short-lived, however, because the main exhibition hall at York needed to be completely emptied in order to replace the roof. A contingent of locomotives and rolling stock was sent to Swindon, until the work was complete as, 'The National Railway Museum on Tour' and a display was mounted in the now defunct 19 Shop of Swindon Works. *City of Truro* entered under her own steam on the evening of 9th April to a champagne toast and fireworks.

It was steamed occasionally outside 19 Shop and made a foray to the Gloucester & Warwickshire Railway's annual gala at Toddington on the weekend of 13-14th October. The Swindon exhibition closed that same month and No. 3440 moved to Bulmer's Railway Centre at Hereford, appearing in two spring open days. The Taff Vale Railway 150 celebrations followed, in June 1991, (held at Cardiff Cathays Wagon Works) and then a move to Bristol for the Bath Road Open Day at the end of the month was successfully undertaken.

Many more events were honoured with the locomotive's presence in 1991 including open days and visits to preserved railway lines.

Return to NRM in early 1992 saw it take part in the National Railway Museum's week of celebrations of 15-20th April and the opening of the new Great Hall to the public.

The seven-year boiler certificate (the main line portion) was by now due to expire and a last main line run was planned for 2nd May. After proceeding to Butterley overnight it went on to Derby from where it hauled an excursion to Paddington, the last steam locomotive to work into the former GWR terminus before rebuilding work started.

There were three years of the boiler certificate left for working on preservation lines and sites and 1992 included a 'West Country Tour' commencing with a display, in steam, outside the Cathedral at Truro during the week of that city's Edwardian Festival. Visits to railways in the region covered the Bodmin & Wenford, the South Devon and the West Somerset. A return to York for static display followed.

Part of the old works at Swindon was rebuilt into the McArthur Glen designer outlet shopping centre and for three years *City of Truro* was on display in the food hall there. It was recalled to York in time for the opening of the new 'The Works' gallery in 1999 and has since been moved into the refurbished NRM workshops for full restoration to working order in time for the hundredth anniversary of the record run of 9th May 1904.

The boiler was removed and left York for specialist restoration and the museum's own expert workshop staff meticulously dismantled and restored the rest. Much was discovered and many repairs undertaken and components replaced. It is no exaggeration to say that completion of the work will have left *City of Truro* in a better condition than at any time since it was in regular day-to-day service back in the 1920s.

This grand old engine was 100 years old in May this year – 2003 – Happy Birthday!

SUGGESTIONS FOR FURTHER READING:

A) The Great Western Railway

E.T. MacDermot: *History of the Great Western Railway, 2 Volumes.* (2nd edition, revised by C.R. Clinker, Ian Allan, London 1964). First published in 1927 this is still the definitive history of the company.

Kevin Robertson & David Abbot: *GWR The Badminton Line – A Portrait of a Railway* (Alan Sutton, Gloucester, 1988). This was a very expensive line to build. Its conception, construction and operation are fully explained.

J. Norris, G. Beale & J. Lewis: *Edwardian Enterprise: A Review of Great Western Railway Development in the First Decade of this Century.* (Wild Swan Publications, Didcot, 1987).

B) G.J. Churchward and G.W. Locomotives

H. Holcroft: *An Outline of Great Western Locomotive Practice 1837-1947*, (Locomotive Publishing Co, Hampton Court, 1957).

J.H. Russell: *A Pictorial Record of Great Western Engines, 2 Volumes.* (Oxford Publishing Co. Oxford, 1975).

Railway Correspondence & Travel Society: *The Locomotives of the Great Western Railway* in 14 Parts (RCTS, between 1951 and 1993). See particularly: *Part Seven, Dean's Larger Tender Engines*, (1954).

Col. H.C.B. Rogers: *G.J. Churchward A Locomotive Biography*, (Allen & Unwin, London, 1975).

C) Great Western 4-4-0 Classes and 'City of Truro

O.S. Nock: *Standard Gauge Great Western 4-4-0s, Part 1: Inside-cylinder Classes 1894-1910* and *Part 2: Counties' to the Close, 1904-1961* (David & Charles, Newton Abbot, 1977 and 1978)

Nigel Harris (ed): *City of Truro : A Locomotive Legend* (Silver Link Publishing, Carnforth, 1985: 2nd edition 1992).

Michael Rutherford : "A John Player Special at York" in *Newsletter of Friends of the National Railway Museum* No. 37 November 1986 pp13-15

ibid "John Player – A Postscript *Newsletter* No. 40 August 1987, pp 6-8

Michael Rutherford: "GWR Double-Framed 4-4-0s" in *Backtrack* Vol 12 No 3 March 1998 pp 153-161

D) Locomotive Performance and Record Runs

O.S. Nock : *Sixty Years of Western Express Running* (Ian Allan, London, 1973)

Charles Rous-Marten : "Railway Speed, The Great Western Railway's Record of Records", in *Railway Magazine* June 1904 p 503.

G.A. Sekon : "Overseas Passenger Traffic at Plymouth (The LSWR's New Arrangements)" in *Railway Magazine* May 1904 p 353.

"Train Speeds : A Revelation", in *GWR Magazine* November 1922 p 500.

Cecil J. Allen : "British Locomotive Practice & Performance" in *Railway Magazine* particularly July, September, October and December 1934.

H.G. Kendal : "What Happened Was This … " in *Railway Magazine*, September 1960, p 656.

John Lewis : "More Light on City of Truro?" in *British Railways Journal* No. 1 October 1983 p 19.

E) Ocean Liners and Mail Traffic

Herbert Russell : "An Ocean 'Special' : An American Mail Boat Train on the Great Western Railway", in *Railway Magazine*, January 1904 p1.

F. Harcourt : "British Oceanic Mail Contracts in the Age of Steam" 1838-1914 in the *Journal of Transport History, 3rd Series,* 1988, Vol 9 No 1 p1.

Ronald Hope : *A New History of British Shipping* (John Murray, London, 1990)

Dennis Griffiths : *Brunel's 'Great Western'* (Patrick Stephens, Wellingborough, 1985)

Arnold Kludas : *Great Passenger Ships of the World, Volume 1, 1858 - 1912* Patrick Stephens, Cambridge, 2nd edition, 1984.

D.G. Hoppins : *Some Notes on the History of the Great Western Docks at Millbay, Plymouth, 1840 to 1932.* (Unpublished typescript, n.d.) Copy held by National Railway Museum Library.

WORKING OF SPECIAL MAIL TRAINS BETWEEN PLYMOUTH AND LONDON.

Distance m.	chs.	Stations.	American Line. S.S. St. Louis, April 9th. Arrive.	Depart.	Time occupied. h. m.	Speed per hour. miles	North German Lloyd. S.S. Kaiser Wilhelm II., April 18th. Arrive.	Depart.	Time occupied. h. m.	Speed per hour. miles	American Line. S.S. St. Paul, April 23rd. Arrive.	Depart.	Time occupied. h. m.	Speed per hour. miles
		Plymouth—Millbay Crossing		a.m. 4.59	- -	—	—	p. m. 4.21	-			p. m. 3.55		
23	79	Totnes	5. 33		- 34	42.69	4. 55		- 34	42.32	4. 25½		- 30½	47.19
8	55	Newton Abbot ...	5 46		- 13	40.09	5. 6		- 11	47.49	4. 36		- 10½	49.64
20	15	Exeter	6.11	6.15	- 25	49.35	5. 29		- 23	52.66	5. 1		- 25	49.35
30	63	Taunton	6. 43		- 28	65.97	5. 58		- 29	63.69	5. 31		- 30	61.57
11	45	Bridgwater	6. 52		- 9	77.07	6. 8		- 10	69.37	5. 41½		- 10	66.07
32	69	Bristol { Pylle Hill ...	—	—	- .	—	—	—	- -	—	—	—	-	—
33	19	Bristol { Temple Meads	7.21	7.29	- 29	68.76	6.39½	6.45	- 31½	63.27	6.11	6.15	- 29½	67.60
34	57	Wootton Bassett { via Badminton	8. 7		- 38	54.81	7. 19		- 34	61.25	6. 51		- 36	57.85
35	36	Wootton Bassett { via Box	—	—	- -	—	—	—	- .	—	—	—	- -	—
5	48	Swindon	8. 13		- 6	56.00	7. 25		- 6	56.00	6. 56½		- 5½	61.09
24	13	Didcot	8. 33		- 20	72.49	7. 45		- 20	72.49	7. 18		- 21½	67.43
17	9	Reading	8 46		- 13	78.91	8. 2		- 17	60.39	7. 33		- 15	68.45
36	0	Paddington	9.17		- 31	69.67	8.34	—	- 32	67.50	8.7	—	- 34	63·53

Stations.	American Line. S.S. Philadelphia, April 30th. Arrive.	Depart.	Time occupied. h. m.	Speed per hour. miles	North German Lloyd. S.S. Kaiser Wilhelm der Grosse, May 2nd. Arrive.	Depart.	Time occupied. h. m.	Speed per hour. miles
Plymouth—Millbay Crossing		p. m. 6.1	- -	—	—	p. m. 12.21	- -	—
Totnes	6. 29		- 28	51.40	12. 49		- 28	51.40
Newton Abbot	6. 38		- 9	57·91	12. 58		- 9	57.91
Exeter	7.1	7.5	- 23	52.65	1. 19		- 21	57.66
Taunton	7. 36		- 31	59.58	1. 49		- 30	61.55
Bridgwater	7. 46		- 10	69.37	2. 0		- 11	63.06
Bristol { Pylle Hill	8.13	8.16	- 27	73.86	2.29	2.31	- 29	68.76
Bristol { Temple Meads	—	—	- -	—	—	—	- -	—
Wootton Bassett { via Badminton	—	—	- -	—	—	—	- -	—
Wootton Bassett { via Box	8. 50		- 34	62.55	3. 5		- 34	62.55
Swindon	8. 55		- 5	67.20	3. 10		- 5	67.20
Didcot	9. 13½		- 18½	78.36	3. 31		- 21	69.03
Reading	9. 27		- 13½	76.06	3. 45½		- 14½	70.81
Paddington	9.55	—	- 28	77.14	4.17	—	- 31½	68.57

Stations.	American Line. S.S. St. Louis, May 7th. Arrive.	Depart.	Time occupied. h. m.	Speed per hour. miles	North German Lloyd. S.S. Kronprinz Wilhelm, May 9th. Arrive. h.m.s.	Depart. h.m.s.	Time occupied. m. s.	Speed per hour. miles
Plymouth—Millbay Crossing	—	a. m. 8.27	- -	—	a. m. —	a. m. 9.23.10	- -	—
Totnes	8. 57		- 30	47.97	—	9.50.49	27 39	52.05
Newton Abbot	9. 7		- 10	52.13	—	9.59.52	9 3	57.59
Exeter	9. 28		- 21	57.68	—	10.22.12	22 20	54·23
Taunton	9. 57		- 29	63.70	—	10.50.1	27 49	66.41
Bridgwater	10. 7		- 10	69.38	—	10.59.24	9 23	73.94
Bristol { Pylle Hill	10.35	1037½	- 28	71.22	11.26.29	11.30.12	27 5	72.80
Bristol { Temple Meads	—	—	- -	—	* Bristol East Depot	11.33.51	3 39	23.63
Wootton Bassett { via Badminton	—	—	- -	—				
Wootton Bassett { via Box	11. 13½		- 36	59.07	† Bath	11.43.50	9 59	60.78
Swindon	11. 19		- 5½	61.09	‡	p.m. 12.9.49	25 59	68.35
Didcot	11. 41		- 22	65.89	—	12.29.20	19 31	74.28
Reading	11. 55		14	73.34	—	12.42.21	13 1	78.88
Paddington	12.28	—	- 33	65.45	Platform	1.9.38	27 17	79.17
					Dead Stop.	1.9.58	From Reading 27 37	

* Distance Pylle Hill to East Depot 1m. 35chs.
† Distance East Depot to Bath 10m. 9chs.
‡ Distance Bath to Swindon 29m. 48chs.

	S.S. St. Louis, April 9th	S.S. Kaiser Wilhelm II., April 18th	S.S. St. Paul, April 23rd	S.S. Philadelphia, April 30th	S.S. Kaiser Wilhelm der Grosse, May 2nd	S.S. St. Louis, May 7th	S.S. Kronprinz Wilhelm, May 9th
Total time occupied ...	4h. 18min.	4h. 13min.	4h. 12min.	3h. 54min.	3h. 56min.	4h. 1min.	hrs. m. sec. Paddington platform, 3 46.28; dead stop 3 46.48
Speed per hour throughout, including stops	57·21 miles.	58·39 miles.	58·58 miles.	63·27 miles.	62·73 miles.	60·86 miles.	65·49 miles.
Speed per hour throughout, excluding stops	60·01 miles.	59·69 miles.	59·52 miles.	65·22 miles.	63·27 miles.	62.03 miles.	66·39 miles.
Load of 8-wheeled Vans from Plymouth ...	5	5	5	4	5	5	5
Load of 8-wheeled Vans from Bristol	3	3	3	2	3	3	4
Engines and Drivers	Plymouth to Exeter, No. 3452, Driver Uren. Exeter to Bristol, No. 3442, Driver Warren. Bristol to Paddington, No. 3066, Driver Edwards.	Plymouth to Bristol, No. 3442, Driver Warren. Bristol to Paddington, No. 3396, Driver Lee.	Plymouth to Bristol, No. 3442, Driver Clements. Bristol to Paddington, No. 3056, Driver T. Burt.	Plymouth to Exeter, No. 3442, Driver Warren. Exeter to Pylle Hill, No. 3052, Driver Killock. Pylle to Paddington, No. 3995, Driver Underhill.	Plymouth to Paddington No. 3437, Driver Millard.	Plymouth to Paddington No. 3442, Driver J. Warren.	Plymouth to Bristol, No. 3440, "City of Truro," Driver Clements. Bristol to Paddington, No. 3065, "Duke of Connaught," Driver Underhill.

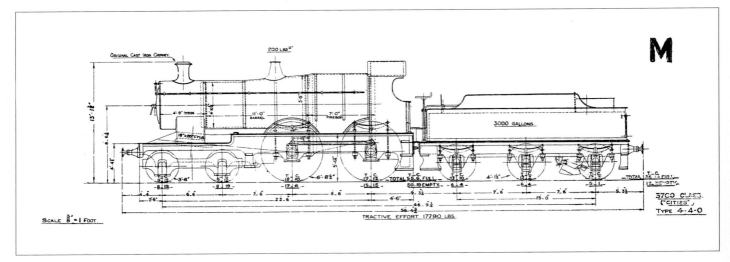

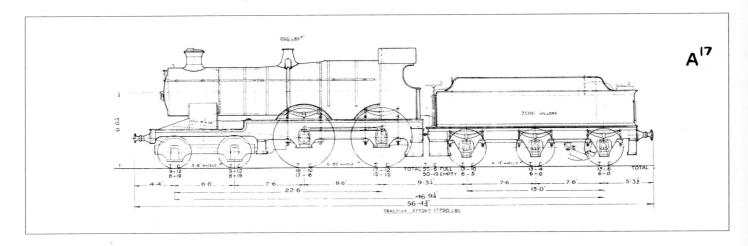

Weight diagrams of 'City' class locomotives:
top: Diagram 4-4-0M as built, non superheated and slide valves.
The 3000 gallon tender shown was invariably a 3500 gallon one,
below: Diagram 4-4-0A.17 as superheated and fitted with piston valves.

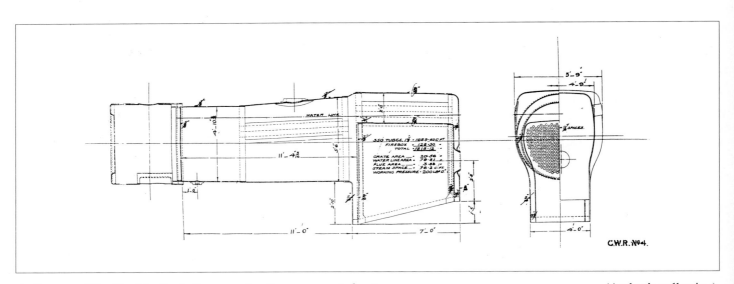

A diagram of the No. 4 boiler before superheating was carried out.   (Author's collection)